The Grand Stories Project

OrangeBooks Publication

1st Floor, Rajhans Arcade, Mall Road, Kohka, Bhilai, Chhattisgarh 490020

Website: **www.orangebooks.in**

First Edition, 2025

ISBN: 978-93-7426-342-6

Price: Rs. 150.00

Printed in India

The Grand Stories Project

Because every grandparent has a story to tell

Sana Gupta

OrangeBooks Publication
www.orangebooks.in

Dedicated To My Future Self

Author's Note

On my balcony sits a family of 20 plants that my nani speaks to every morning. In my jewellery box - ever so carefully placed - are pearl drop earrings, gifted to me by my grandmother. On my pin board are 3 letters, written in cursive, from my dadoo to his pen pal.

In my heart? These are stories that I discovered through many conversations. Each story is from a grandparent, mine or others' - the simplicity and beauty of which has given me comfort during late-night exam preparations, stressful days and off moods.

Perhaps, these are simply glimpses and contours of a deeper personal story for each grandparent. I recognise this is a beginning. But my wish is that we find some inspiration from this short book to discover the life stories around us.

My grandparents' souls are scattered everywhere - my room, the dining table where a fat bottle of achaar sits, and my soul - where they will be forever etched in times of doubt.

I want to share that joy with more people. Not everyone is lucky enough to be force - fed badam and dahi before exams and to have their nazar spontaneously taken off. I have learnt a lot from my grandparents and seniors in general - I hope to share that in this short book.

About the Author

Sana is a young writer who believes in storytelling can bridge generations. What began as heartfelt conversations with grandparents grew into The Grand Stories Project - her first collection of true-life stories celebrating courage, love, and beauty in everyday lives. Through #MyGrandStory, she invites readers and hopes to spark a movement to share family stories and honour the elders who shaped them. Thoughtful, bright, and full of curiosity, Sana carries a storyteller's heart and a budding grandparent's wisdom within her.

Kusum Sharma

'Munni'

Who finds joy in the little things

As a child, a high-school graduate and then a Lucknow University Grad, Kusum ('Munni') Sharma had mapped out her life; a perfect, unwavering and solidified bullet pointed list:

* A happy marriage
* A big family
* Daily bridge
* An enviable rose garden
* And... no career plans.

And eventually, this plan panned out. She married at 25 to an engineer she learnt to love, raised an incredibly bright kid and a white-picket-fenced garden.

As her child, Ritu, grew up, learning alphabets and numbers from her mother, Kusum sparked and ignited a love for teaching in herself - a career, a different life path that she never planned to take up. Untrained but eager, she fought and earned a job teaching and was eventually made the head of junior school.

"Rona dhona nahi chahiye. Take chances."

As a lover of gardening – an interest she picked up from her father – Kusum, coincidentally, a name meaning 'flower' – fostered flowers, fruit trees and an abundance of greenery.

One bright and humid day, her treasured rose patch basked in the golden haze of the sun; its fragrance inviting and sight alluring. Though soon, a wandering herd of stray cows passed by, trampling the patch and chewing on each and every radiant rose petal.

Kusum cried for days, staring at the empty dirt patch, strewn with broken stems and wilted leaves after years of growth and care.

But she, herself, did not remain wilted. She reset herself, growing marigolds, tulips and lilies. Later, she moved, leaving behind her garden in Roorkee. Her old garden, though now just a sunlit patch of memory, helped her carry her memories and passion to new places.

Today, she is the proud owner of a fenced, beautiful garden, adorned with flowers of all kinds, and seeds that are yet to grow.

When Kusum got her first teaching job at a convent school, she was proud and undeniably nervous. On her very first day, her boss, A tall lady with thin-rimmed glasses, namely Mrs. Sinha, looked over her pristine lesson plan notes and told her, “You’ll need to stop writing in print. We teach in cursive.”

Cursive felt stiff, foreign. But she didn’t protest. The same day, she bought a notebook - a distinct, four-lined notebook.

The next day, she marched into Mrs. Sinha’s office and asked her to write a sentence there. Any sentence, in the cursive that was demanded and expected. And so, it was written.

After days and weeks of wobbly writing and empty ink bottles, that cursive handwriting was achieved. A very small change that required a great deal of effort, and paid off.

Her pupils called on her as their favourite teacher.

Two sisters - Kusum and Kumud - were near polar opposites growing up. Kusum was a self-proclaimed 'Hungama-maker'; a tomboy who started her mornings by climbing mango trees, playing 'Kancha' and returning a ruffian, hair dishevelled and clothes dirty.

On the other hand, her sister, Kumud, was more 'reserved and sober' (per Kusum's words), preferring to spend her time reading, studying and seeking intellectual stimulation. Despite these contrasting characteristics, they grew up incredibly close and are still found giggling away in a corner at family gatherings, as sisters do.

Now Dr Kumud holds a PhD in women's development studies, and is still highly sought after for her work and voice in her field. Always up for a social or political debate, she prefers spending her evenings with a cup of tea, Scrabble or perhaps a poetry book. Kusum now spends her time gardening, prescribing kitchen 'nuskhe' for small ailments and indulging in Sher-O-Shayari. The sisters are as close as ever.

It may be expected for one's childhood to be a warm, fuzzy haze of memories, though Kusum remembers it distinctly. She, along with the entire house, would wake up like clockwork at 7am.

The morning was always to be started with dry fruits - a mix of almonds, walnuts and damp raisins (A favourite '*kishmish*'). After this, it was either a hearty meal with *Gajar Ka Halwa* or *Puri Aloo;* heavenly smells that would waft throughout the large, vast house.

After a relatively slow morning, badminton was the perfect way to speed it up. Freshly cut grass, chappals and a white feathery shuttlecock to wake everyone up, of which Kusum was a consistent champion.

Though arthritis does not permit her to play badminton anymore, she stays consistently active with morning walks and yoga. Of course, the dry fruits are still considered paramount; a cold, a headache and the slightest itch is blamed on a lack of *badam* consumption. Music and books, as she says, will "always accompany her."

C.P Gupta

'Dada'

Who has never faltered with his discipline, reliability and generosity

The route was simple enough — Delhi to Chandigarh, Chandigarh to Jammu, then finally Srinagar. A path flown many times before, under skies both clear and chaotic. That day, though, there was haze. And rain. And a thick layer of clouds that seemed to follow them past Chandigarh. Somewhere left of Jammu, visibility disappeared altogether.

When nothing was visible anymore — not land, not light — the pilot called radar. A voice responded: "Turn right by 10 degrees." But the map showed hills to the right. Still, they turned. Then came the second instruction: "Descend for landing."

From above, the runway came into view — flat and clear, exactly what they were hoping for. But as they neared it, it became obvious that something was off. It wasn't Jammu. It was Pakistan.

Jammu, for one, doesn't have a hangar. This one did.

By then, their communications had been intercepted. Officials had started listening. And on the other side of the border, fighter jets were being prepared. The pilot didn't wait for confirmation. He pulled up.

They flew higher, into the clouds again — not sure where exactly they were, just certain of where they shouldn't be. The passengers reached Jammu safely.

At 25, C.P. Gupta interviewed to be a pilot in the Indian Air Force, to serve his country – a dream he had held since the days he milked cows and played 'Gulli Danda' and 'Bantey'.

In a slick suit with sweaty palms, he walked into the interview room, where three questions came his way:

"What is the value of zero?"

"What is the thickness of a wicket in millimetres?"

and "What were the contents of the Hindustan Times political section on the 19th of November?"

His answer to all was quick, simple and blunt. "I don't know". They laughed, stared, looked confused, and he walked out with a heavy sense of doubt weighing on his shoulders.

Months later, he got the job. Why? One of the interviewers told him later that indeed the panel was divided and his candidature was heavily debated. What ultimately worked in his favour was his honesty and that he gave the answers without a moment's hesitation. That showed the kind of alertness that every pilot needs when they need to make decisions in a split second.

He is now a proud ex-aviator of the Indian Air Force. His confidence in his decisions and his generosity of spirit have remained with him.

Once, he was driving a commercial plane, per usual - the sky was clear, the engine was running, and the destination was close. Suddenly, a large vulture flew at the screen. One of the engines was blown, but which one?

The vulture crashed on the left– Captain Chander's co-pilot insisted on switching off the left engine. However, there was a shadow of doubt– if, in fact, the right engine was blown, switching off the left engine would cause a crash.

The clock was ticking. This decision had to be taken within a few seconds, or a crash would happen anyway. Turns out, the right engine was blown. The descent was difficult, but achieved. After a lengthy round of questioning by ground patrol, his efforts were briefly applauded, and he headed on home.

Never doubt your gut.

The late 70s and 80s were good times, and the job of a commercial pilot was enviable as he and the family travelled to distant places and stayed in the best of hotels. C.P. remained his own person, authentic and straightforward. Well, in one of those hotels, he came up the elevator with someone whom he thought was familiar. He squinted and looked again, but he could not identify him. Finally, he asked, "Sorry, but I might have seen you somewhere." Turns out that 'familiar face' was the biggest actor of the time, none other than Amitabh Bachchan! The ribbing from the family continues to this day.

A friend's friend and someone who was known to speak his mind fearlessly, he then stood and won the election to become the Pilot's Union president. His quotes and interviews got published in the papers, and the decision makers in aviation sought his views. When C.P. looks back at life, he always says that for someone who started his work life at a construction site as a supervisor, destiny indeed sprinkled some magic, and for that, he will always be grateful to the Almighty.

C.P. grew up as a kid in the 1940s and 1950s, where his pocket money consisted of 10 paisa (1/10th of a rupee) every week. With this, he'd purchase and munch a pocket full of peanuts throughout the week.

Now, a granddad who hands out wads of cash to his grandies at every request and whim, his sole piece of financial advice is to know how to save, but also know how to spend. Always remain pragmatic while spending on yourself, and enjoy all the little things you get.

Sudarshan Mohini Gupta

“The Original LinkedIn”

She who could do anything she put her mind to

mutton curry

Even as a homemaker and caretaker of 3 'charming but overactive' kids, Sudarshan Mohini didn't find she had enough to do. So, even in times where women were not actively encouraged to go down career-oriented paths as such, she founded and ran multiple successful businesses.

The first was an export business she jointly operated with another lady, Ms. Daisy, and the second– one she holds extremely close to her heart– was that of making children's clothing. She would cut up gorgeous fabrics - silk, cotton, lace - and train underprivileged women near her house to stitch them, providing them with livelihoods. On any given rainy afternoon, even now, you can find her sipping a cup of chai on the balcony, adorning a gorgeous floral saree and a self-made shawl.

Her intricate designs are still worn to this day, not only by her kids, grandkids and past customers, but modelled by herself. Her resourcefulness and generosity of time were unparalleled. Much before wedding planners came into vogue, Mohini was the default go-to organiser for every wedding in the extended family. From knowing exactly where and what to buy, to being the sought - after advisor, Mohini was at the helm of large family functions. Her mental yellow pages and phone diary could unlock a whole world. She was always a call away and ever ready to drive off in her car to help anyone who called.

Not to mention that her business spirit still lives on, as she thrives watching the ups and downs of the stock market. One of the early investors in the 1990s, when most of India still believed only in fixed deposits, Mohini actively filled up physical forms to apply for IPOs. The thrill and zeal for the stock market never dimmed, and the drone of CNBC TV 18 can still be heard in the house from 9 am to 3.30 PM. Generous with stock tips and widely believed by the family to be the lucky one, many people have been given the 'must buys.' One of the oldest clients of the local brokerage, she is a VIP customer for whom the runner is still sent home to pick up the instructions.

Stories from the partition and her ancestral house at Lahore always bring a lump to her throat. Tucked away carefully in the recesses of her cupboard is a hand - embroidered tablecloth from her mother, who she lost when she was only 4 years old. Growing up in a loving joint family, she spent her childhood in the hills of Himachal and later became a librarian who was admired for her impeccably tied saris, quiet nature and pencil heels.

In the 1960s, before quirky baking websites and recipes specific to the teaspoon took over, Sudarshan Mohini, in pristine, beautiful cursive, compiled a list of all of her famous, inimitable recipes – Mutton Curry, Suji Ka Halwa, Mango Achaar, and so much more. These dishes, copied to this day by kids and grandkids alike, are treasured and heartily eaten.

In fact, her impeccable taste not only in food, but in clothes, helps her family to this day. Every day, for the past 30 years, by 9 am, she has been seen to be perfectly dressed in Georgette sarees, adorning her favourite pearl necklace and earrings. Perhaps this is why she has been the longstanding assistant shopper in the family, helping find fabrics and linings for wedding outfits in the nooks and crannies of bazaars and markets.

Today, she holds very few regrets. Though one of the greatest losses she mourns is her inability to wear heels.

Dr Kumud Sharma

She who absorbs and radiates knowledge

As a little girl with a love for the humanities and a district education officer as a dad, Kumud would move around a lot. Once she finished the 10th grade– amongst the top of her class– her father was posted in a small city where there were no girls' institutions. As her desperation to grip a pencil and scrawl notes in a notebook grew, her restlessness grew too.

Her father pushed the principal of a local school to incorporate a co-ed system, refusing to let his daughter, hungry for knowledge, sit at home. After much debate, the system was introduced, and out of a class of 90, only 4 girls sat behind benches, eagerly writing down everything the teachers had to say.

She distinctly remembers that as more girls started to join the school, the daughter of a dancer was refused admission. Her father, again, pushed for her right to education that transcends caste and gender.

After her post-graduation, she stayed on at the university to do a PhD. Three years passed in a blink — lectures, library afternoons, and long nights bent over drafts. The work felt ordinary then; only years later did she look back and realise it was the start of a career she never planned. During this gruelling research period, as if she didn't have enough on her plate, she decided she was obliged to prepare for the UPSC exam and learn a new language.

When the newly crowned Dr. moved to Jaipur after getting married, she handed in her resignation for a teaching job she loved. It felt like the sensible thing to do. But a few months into house-hunting and hosting visitors, she wished she'd held on to her post. That was the last time she ever left a job halfway.

A year later, she was invited to join the Committee on the Status of Women in India. Back then, nobody thought women's research was serious work. The committee changed that — her report was passed from desk to desk, cited in policy, and fifty years on, after changing thousands of lives and female careers, it was celebrated at a special event this March. The Indian Council of Social Science Research funded its first - ever project on women's studies because of it. Then they set up a centre. It was 1975, the National Year for Women, and for the next decade, she learned as much as she taught.

In her reticent, self-effacing way, she will typically forget to mention the publication of several books. Several. To this day, she speaks out to the public about her work and women's issues in India, dressed in chiffon or silk sarees with perfectly coiffed hair.

Retirement is seen to be a time of complete relaxation after years of hard work, but Dr. Sharma has much to show for it. Yes, she still is publishing research and writing papers. Always up for a spirited discussion, dinner conversations with the next generation are full of counter arguments, wit and at times words people have to ask the meaning of!

Her love for reading has gone beyond literature, having read crime thrillers, recommendations from her grandkids, Sher O Shaayari, psychology, poetry and personal favourites like "Who Moved My Cheese?". A love for music and theatre is also potent– on any given afternoon, she can be seen with digital Scrabble in hand, once again beating the computer at it, and then lost in some Indian classical.

Rekha Aggarwal

'Pammi'

She who is the best company

In a family where everyone was physics-oriented, it was hardly a surprise that all paths led to numbers and experiments. The ladies pursued MScs, the brothers went into engineering. Allegedly, she was brilliant in math and science but hopeless at history and literature. Humanities felt like a different language altogether.

When they shifted to another area mid-session, Pammi's history teacher gave her a really hard time, describing her as hopeless to the principal, a math teacher. In his class, Pammi always raised her hand first, and so he knew: this child was very far from hopeless.

Years later, she was teaching physics in those same classrooms. When she got children, she wanted to focus on raising them and prayed for her husband's salary to simply double. And sure enough, one day that happened — and she has cherished every moment with her kids.

Once her kids grew up and settled, she joined in on a business operation, and so eventually, "career" and "family" balanced themselves perfectly.

Pammi was only 17 with a backpack full of books and pens, no cell phone and no accompaniment, when she embarked on a journey from Nainital to Bareilly and then Dehradun.

Reaching Bareilly was a breeze. Post this, however, this route of travel was nothing short of treacherous. Heavy rains and thunderstorms meant that trains were delayed to the next day. She stood on the platform, clueless. She had nowhere to stay overnight. What was she to do?

A few strangers helped. A man told her where to go. Someone suggested Haridwar. Someone offered space under an umbrella.

Eventually, she caught a train to Haridwar, then a bus. Long, bumpy ride, half-soaked and hungry. But she reached. Late at night, in a new city, she stepped off the bus and kept walking.

There was no one to call to say "I'm okay." No one said "You did well." But she knew it anyway. She said this was her first story of absolute independence– finding support from strangers and finding faith in herself.

She never grew up in apartments. Just open houses, open yards, and entire days spent playing outside. Jump rope, *stapoo*, climbing things she wasn't supposed to. "Girlish games, boyish games" — whatever that meant. Vijay, her younger brother, was always around.

She was five or six, already obsessed with stories. Listening, reading, imagining — all of it. If someone asked, *"Do you want to hear a story?"* she was there before they finished the question.

That day, she was in the living room. The sofa in their house had removable cushions. That's what she was used to. Soft seat, cushion off, a little dip — normal.

So, when someone pulled out a chair for her — one with just the wooden frame and no seat — she was suspicious. Thought they were trying to prank her. So, she sat on the other chair, the "safe" one.

She fell straight through it.

And instead of crying, she laughed. Hard. Everyone did. She says this was one of her best memories of her childhood.

Neerja Sawhney

She who finds joy in simplicity

Neerja distinctly remembers having a natural talent for table tennis, perhaps as a result of her mom's insistence but also because it was a release.

As a shy, quiet and somewhat reserved teenage girl, performing under pressure was foreign and new to her, so when she participated in a table tennis tournament and won runner-up, she was elated. Bits of applause from classmates and adults, a small golden trophy and a pat on the back were great– but what stuck with her was the little 2 by 4 cm column that said: 'Neerja Sawhney: Runner up.'

In a girls' convent, where young women were told that they were better off seen than heard, and were forced into a mould of being submissive and quiet, Neerja looked at that minuscule column every day– and felt a sense of freedom and accomplishment. At 60, she is still as active as ever - golf and brunch with 'her girls' are part of her everyday routine. They call their group the 'Gulaab Gang.'

Picking and choosing the right career path is always daunting, and indeed, Neerja came to realise this. As somewhat of a shy, timid and talented individual, she started as a copywriter in her early career. However, later on, a newer, much more dynamic opportunity presented itself: to get into corporate training– speaking in front of latte-drinking, intimidating 20 - somethings and big officials in suits. After much debate, she went for it.

After a few weeks of training and anxiety-ridden sleepless nights, Neerja was called in to host her first corporate training session. The night prior wasn't restful: insomnia, sweaty palms and as stated by her, "a lot of perspiration" played into the night.

When she woke up and drove to the job site, there was no choice but to start; so she did. Though it wasn't a resounding success or a massive breakthrough moment out of that reserved, rigid shell, she absolutely did it, and when it was over, she felt a million times lighter. Not only that, but she found a part of herself that she never knew was there. Gradually, she built her confidence and is now operating an educational YouTube channel for kids.

"Yes, this may sound like a boilerplate motivational book but believe in yourself. Really, really believe in yourself. No one else will do it for you."

Sharmilla Ghosh

She who finds joy in giving back, and looking good

Mrs. Sharmilla, though was oblivious to this sentiment herself, makes an impression. Adorned in gorgeous golden jewellery, chiffon sarees and bedazzled juttis, one can't help but stop, stare and go on with their day. However, many couldn't help but ask: "Where is that saree from?"

And from this question stemmed a business. Now, Sharmilla goes from place to place in India: Odisha, Delhi, Ahmedabad, and handpicks boutique pieces for her curious admirers, exporting them out of Gurgaon.

Her style mantras, as very clearly stated, consist of 4 elements: Age, time, season, and (as was added on a later phone call) occasion. Other cardinal rules she lives by? The daytime is for lighter colours, the nighttime for darker; but white? White is always in style.

She is undeniably stylish– but her sources of joy go beyond clothes. As a dedicated Buddhist with mantras, she has lived through hard times of unemployment and uncertainty– an "I will win" chant fulfils and comforts her.

What brings her joy even more is giving back to society: feeding stray dogs, funding orphanages, schools and the underprivileged. She vows to continue this for the rest of her life.

As a kid, she would constantly get *bukhaars* – though the burning forehead and constant fatigue wasn't fun, it was a free pass out of dull events and into absolute maternal care: foot massages, cold mangos and the works.

However, one fever couldn't have come at a worse time. It was her *maamaa's* wedding, and no fever was going to stop her from dancing her little heart out. She masterfully hid her coughs and sneezes from her mom, in collaboration with her partners in crime: her cousins. They'd sneakily give her medicine, ban her from her beloved iced teas and covertly mix cough syrup in her water. It is one of her fondest childhood memories– and she holds it dear to this day.

Anita Khanna

She shows how it all gets done

business
ideas

Anita simply cannot pick a favorite memory of her childhood - she remembers it all too fondly. She grew up in cantonments, the kind of places with open skies, quiet discipline, and not a lot of noise. Her days were mostly spent outdoors, goofing around with her siblings. Whether it had been badminton in the club or bickering over table tennis, the sun always gleamed, the trees always swayed, and the hills always looked over them.

There wasn't much pressure. No rigorous, tight school routine; just her elder brother, younger sister and neighbour's kids who came and went along like family.

This spirit of sports and family has never left Anita. Today, she spends her time playing golf and bridge – "each an exercise of the body and soul", she says. Each game played, as her friends say, has her grace, touch of style and her inimitable competitive spirit. She's also still in touch with her siblings, though they are on opposite ends of the world. The bickering, joking and teasing continue to this day.

Anita, in her 20s, made the bold move to leave the national bank where she worked. However, there was no backup plan; no alternative in mind.

She did have a friend in advertising. This friendship and her entrepreneurial spirit meant daily discussions on new business ideas. After brainstorming through hundreds of ideas - some bad, some good- she arrived at something.

It was the mid - 70s, and she kept hearing the term "Phototype setting" - agencies lining up to get it done - but no one really knew how to do it fast or well. So she figured it out, and how. Started small, got it up and running, and sold it a while later. But the entrepreneurial fire had been lit, along with a vibrant, stylish personality. Both have lasted through the years.

Later, Anita opened a leather factory. Eventually began distribution for Hidesign, a well - known brand. In summary: work was constant, but not without a bubbly dose of socialising, good times and as her friends confirm, looking like a diva.

She stopped working fifteen years ago. But back then, she says, she would've done anything that felt new. She just needed something to break the monotony. Turns out, that was simply enough to sparkle.

… and the stories will continue